Spinach Recipes You'll Want To Make Forever

Lowri .X Sumner

Introduction

This book offers a diverse collection of culinary delights showcasing the versatility and nutritional benefits of spinach. The recipes span various categories, allowing spinach enthusiasts to explore new and enticing ways to incorporate this leafy green into their meals.

The journey begins with a selection of hearty soups, including the rich and flavorful "Mushroom and Spinach Soup," the velvety "Creamy Spinach Soup," and the unique "Lentil and Spinach Soup with Chopped Pork Rind." The soup section also features international influences with recipes like "Chinese-Style Spinach and Mushroom Soup" and "Tuscan Soup."

Moving on to pies, bread, and pancakes, the book introduces tempting options such as "Spanakopita (Greek Spinach Pie)," "Cheesy Mushroom, Pancetta, and Spinach Pancakes," and "Spinach and Ricotta Ham Rolls." These recipes showcase the delightful pairing of spinach with various ingredients, creating satisfying and flavorful dishes.

In the mains section, the book explores a variety of dishes, from the elegant "Marinated Steak with Spinach and Feta Cheese Roulades" to the comforting "Chicken Roulade with Cheddar and Spinach." There's something for every palate, including seafood lovers with the enticing "Seafood and Spinach Risotto."

Salads are not overlooked, with vibrant and refreshing options like "Spinach and Mango Salad," "Asian Spinach Salad with Chicken, Mushrooms, Peppers, and Almond," and "Warm Beet and Spinach Salad." These salads showcase the balance of flavors and textures that spinach can bring to a dish.

The smoothie section introduces creative and nutritious blends, such as the "Simple Banana Spinach Smoothie" and the "Peanut Butter Banana Spinach Smoothie," providing a delicious way to incorporate spinach into a daily routine.

To add a touch of freshness to summer, the book includes a recipe for "Basil and Spinach Summer Pesto," offering a versatile sauce that can elevate a variety of dishes.

With a diverse range of recipes, this book invites readers to explore the culinary possibilities of spinach and enjoy its nutritional benefits in a variety of delightful dishes.

Contents

.

<u>Soups</u>

Mushroom and Spinach Soup

Shiitake is a mushroom that is very flavorful and gives its dish a 'classy' presentation. This recipe is very easy to make and won't need much of your time, though you need to soak the mushrooms beforehand. Sauté everything, add a thickener and add the stock and you've got soup!

Yields: Makes 6 servings

Ingredients:
3 tablespoon Butter
4 tablespoon Flour
2 med onions, chopped
2 cloves Garlic, minced
6 Shitake mushrooms, minced
3 onion leeks, chopped
Spinach leaves, cut Chiffonade
Salt and Pepper
8 cups Chicken stock
Croutons

Method of Preparation:

1. Soak your mushroom 1 hour before cooking. Do not discard the liquid.
2. In a saucepan, heat the butter and sauté the onions and garlic but do not brown. Add flour and pour in the chicken stock and the liquid from the soaked mushrooms. Add minced shiitake mushrooms and bring to a boil. Once it has thickened, add the Spinach and immediately turn off the heat.

.   3. Upon serving, put some chopped onion leeks and croutons if desired.

Creamy Spinach Soup

This hearty recipe is traditional for family gatherings or for supper. Growing up as a child, this is one of the comfort food I love best. Its chunkiness is filling, its creaminess is satisfying…you won't even need a main course to fill you up.

Yields: Serves 6.

Ingredients:
6 tablespoons butter
4 tablespoon flour
8 cups chicken stock
1 medium onion, finely chopped
Boiled potatoes, coarsely mashed
1 stalk celery, finely chopped
Fresh Spinach, washed
1/2 cup heavy cream
Salt
Ground Pepper
Garlic French Bread

Garlic French Bread
3 French Bread slices
3 tablespoons butter,
Garlic, minced
Parsley, chopped

Method of Preparation:
Garlic French Bread
1.   Mix 3 tablespoons butter, garlic and parsley in a container and spread to French bread slices. Put in the oven for 7-10 minutes until toasted.

Soup

2.   In a saucepan, mix in butter and sauté onions until caramelized over medium heat. Add in flour stirring constantly and pour in chicken stock

3.   Add the potatoes and celery, simmer for 5 mins

4.   Pour in heavy cream and simmer another for 3 minutes.

5.   Adjust consistency by adding flour into cold water (if needed) to make the soup thicker.

6.   Add the Spinach leaves.

7.   Adjust Salt and pepper to taste.

8.   Serve with Garlic French Bread

Pureed Potato, Spinach & Leek Soup

Potato serves as a thickening agent when pureed. When done in an immersion blender, it will give such a smooth and creamy outcome when blended thoroughly. Added leeks and the sherry wine would give a twist to this all-time favorite family recipe.

Yield: Serves 4

Ingredients:
2 tablespoons unsalted butter
1 onion, cut into 1/2-inch pieces
3 garlic cloves, minced
5 small potatoes, peeled and cut into 1/2-inch pieces
1/4 cup dry sherry or white wine
2 cans chicken broth
1 cup water
2 bunches spinach, leaves rinsed
Leeks, washed and chopped
Coarse salt and freshly ground pepper

Method of Preparation:

1. Heat butter in a saucepan. Add onion, garlic and potatoes.
2. Pour in sherry wine to evaporate the alcohol then pour in Chicken stock.
3. Simmer for 10 minutes until potatoes are very tender
4. Stir in Spinach for 1 minute and put contents in a food processor.
5. Puree everything working in batches so as not to spill anything.
6. Return mixture in saucepan to season with salt and pepper. Adjust according to taste.
7. Garnish with some remaining leeks then serve.

Spinach and Onion soup with Tomato Crostini

A restaurant-style soup can be done in the comforts of your home in no time. The Tomato Crostini adds a little 'spice' to this traditional soup and adds color to it. Most often, the crostini is served floating in the soup which makes it more exciting.

Yield: Serves 6

Ingredients:
4 ¼ cup (1 liter) vegetable stock
1 oz (30 g) butter
1 tbsp extra virgin olive oil
3 large onions, thinly sliced
1 tsp sugar
2 garlic cloves, chopped
1 liter vegetable stock
4 oz (115 g) broccoli, finely chopped
4 oz (115 g) spinach leaves, cut chiffonade
salt and pepper

Tomato Crostini
8 thick slices of French bread
1 garlic clove, halved
2 tsp tomato purée
2 tomatoes, each cut into 8 wedges
1 oz (30 g) Parmesan cheese, freshly grated

Method of Preparation:

1. Prepare bread slices by spreading the tomato puree on the bread.
2. Rub garlic to induce flavor and place tomato slices on top before sprinkling Parmesan cheese.
3. Grill in a pan until bread is toasted.

4. Heat butter and olive oil in a saucepan and sauté onions until transparent.
5. Add in sugar and sauté a little bit more until onions are caramelized.
6. Pour in Vegetable stock and stir. Bring to a boil before adding the Broccoli.
7. Once Broccoli is tender, add in the Spinach and simmer for 1 more minute.
8. Float the Crostini before serving in a soup bowl.

Lentil and Spinach Soup with Chopped Pork Rind

Lentils are a good source of Protein, and with added Spinach, makes it doubly nutritious. Some health conscious would set the Pork Rind aside but if you want to go an extra mile, garnish your soup with chopped Crispy Pork Rinds and indulge. Good for those evenings when you feel empty on your tummy. This recipe will fill you up.

Yield: Serves 4

Ingredients:
4.5 oz dry green lentils, soaked overnight for easy cooking
1 tablespoon olive oil
1 medium onion, chopped
5 cups water or vegetable stock if available.
Fresh spinach, chopped. Set aside a little for garnish
3 tablespoons lemon juice
Salt
1 tablespoon light soy sauce
Ground Pepper
Crispy Pork Rinds (optional)

Method of Preparation:

1. Pork Rinds can be bought cooked in groceries or you can do it at home by deep frying pork belly. Add cornstarch, Salt and Pepper before deep frying to add a little crisp. When done, chop and set aside for garnish.
2. Heat Olive oil in a saucepan and add onions. Sauté until transparent and add lentils.
3. Pour in water or stock and bring to a boil. Simmer for 50 minutes to 1 hour until lentils are ready.

4. Add fresh Spinach and simmer for another minute or two. Adjust seasoning.
5. Ladle in a soup bowl and garnish with chopped Pork Rinds and some finely chopped spinach. Squeeze in Lemon for added flavor.

Tuscan Soup

The sausage originally came from Tuscany and is used in many dishes since the 16th century. This soup has meat and vegetable which makes it balanced. This is a delicious milky recipe and only takes less than 30 minutes to prepare.

Yield: Serves 6

Ingredients:
6 cups chicken broth or vegetable stock
1 onion, finely chopped
2 tablespoons olive oil
A bunch fresh spinach, washed and chopped
3 links spicy Italian sausage, casing removed
3 large potatoes, cubed and soaked in water
1/4 cup evaporated milk
Salt
Freshly ground black pepper

Method of Preparation:

1. In a saucepan, heat olive oil and add onions. Fry until transparent.
2. Then add the sausage meat. Fry until medium brown.
3. Add the potatoes. Wait for 5 minutes and add the stock. Bring to a boil.
4. Once potatoes are tender, add the evaporated milk and spinach.
5. Season with salt and pepper to taste.

Spinach Tortellini Soup

Tortellini is ring-shaped pasta/dumpling and its cheesiness adds richness to the soup. Add the spinach and basil, and then you got one healthy soup.

Yield: Serves 4

Ingredients:
3 cups chicken broth
½ cup water
A bunch of chopped spinach
9 oz cheese tortellini
1/4 tablespoon dried basil
1/4 tablespoon garlic powder
salt and pepper to taste

Method of Preparation:

1. In a saucepan, heat the chicken broth and bring it to a boil.
2. Add the tortellini. Simmer for 5 minutes until done then add Spinach.
3. Season with salt, pepper, basil and garlic powder.

Curried Spinach Soup

A beautifully blended pureed spinach soup with a touch of curry and sour cream. You can coarsely blend the ingredients to make it a bit chunky or puree well to make it smooth. Add 1 tablespoon lemon to make it citrusy.

Yield: Serves 4

Ingredients:
1 large potato, cubed
4 tablespoons olive oil
1/2 cup chopped green onions
12 cups spinach - rinsed, stemmed, and dried
1/3 cup all-purpose flour
2 teaspoons curry powder
4 cups chicken stock
1 tablespoon lemon juice
1 carton nonfat sour cream (8 ounce)
Salt and pepper

Method of Preparation:

1. In a saucepan, heat olive oil and sauté the green onions and potatoes.
2. Add in the curry powder and flour.
3. When potatoes are halfway done, add the stock and then the spinach and let it simmer for 2 minutes.
4. Transfer contents in a food processor and puree.
5. Once done, transfer contents into the saucepan and adjust seasoning.
6. Add in the lemon juice.
7. In a soup bowl, spoon in 1 tablespoon sour cream and ladle the soup into the bowl or top the sour crème into the soup.

Chinese-Style Spinach and Mushroom Soup

An exciting and flavorful soup with a touch from the East is what this is all about. You won't need a main course to fill you up, this soup is chunky filled with tofu and mushrooms, and it's very nutritious too!

Yield: Serves 6

Ingredients:
5 cups vegetable broth
5 oz spinach leaves, washed and stemmed
1 1/2 cups water
4 ounces thinly sliced mushrooms
2 tablespoons soy sauce
2 tablespoons rice vinegar
2 tablespoon oriental sesame oil
2 tablespoon minced garlic
1 tablespoon minced peeled fresh ginger
4 oz thinly sliced mushrooms
1/2 pound firm tofu, cut into 1/2-inch pieces
3 green onions, chopped

Method of Preparation:

1. In a medium stock pot, combine vegetable broth, water, soy sauce, rice vinegar, sesame oil, ginger and garlic. Bring to a boil.
2. Add the mushrooms and simmer for 5 minutes.
3. Then add the tofu, simmer for 2 minutes then add the spinach.
4. Before serving, sprinkle green onions to add freshness to the soup.

Spinach Egg Drop Soup

An easy recipe that only uses spinach and egg as its main ingredient. The flavor of the soup lies on the richness of the stock. Garnish with mint or parsley before serving.

Yield: Serves 6

Ingredients:
6 cups chicken broth
A handful of fresh spinach
2 eggs, lightly beaten
2 tbsp soy sauce
1 tsp sugar
2 green onions, chopped
Pepper (optional)
Mint or parsley (optional) for garnish

Method of Preparation:

1. In a medium stockpot, bring stock to a boil.
2. Add the soy sauce, green onions and sugar.
3. Add the egg, stirring it for 1 minute. Remove from heat.
4. Ladle in soup in soup bowl with spinach at the bottom. Garnish with mint or parsley.

Pies/Breads/Pancakes

Spinach and Ricotta Ham Rolls

Unlike the typical rolls, this recipe uses ham instead of dough which makes it more tempting. Rolled to perfection to make one sumptuous dinner or lunch. Scoop mashed potato and your favorite gravy on the side to make a meal. Invite friends and loved ones over for lunch or dinner and enjoy this savory dish.

Yield: Serves 4

Ingredients:
8 large slices ham
9 oz ricotta cheese
1 can sour cream, set aside 4 tablespoons
1 egg, beaten lightly
1 small onion, finely chopped
A bunch of cooked, well drained spinach
pinch of nutmeg
salt and pepper to taste
1 can or 1 cup cream of mushroom soup
1 tablespoon Mustard
Parsley, chopped

Method of Preparation:

1. Preheat oven to 355 F (180 C).
2. Mix all ingredients in a bowl excluding 4 tablespoons of soured cream and mushroom soup.
3. Spread 2-3 tablespoonfuls onto ham and roll. Place in a baking dish until full.
4. In a bowl, combine cream of mushroom soup and soured cream. Mix evenly. Add water if needed but don't overdo it. Make sure solution is thick enough to cover the baking pan.
5. Bake for 15-20 minutes.

6. Garnish with fresh parsley before serving.

Spanakopita (Greek Spinach Pie)

This traditional Greek Pie is overflowing with nutrients and will simply awaken your taste buds. The simple ingredients are easy to find, maybe you won't need to go to your local supermarket to find one. Also easy to make and won't take much of your time. Baked to perfection until crispy and you'll keep coming back for more.

Yield: Serves 5

Ingredients:
1 large onion, chopped
1 bunch spring onions, chopped
2 lb + 3 oz spinach, rinsed and chopped
1 oz chopped fresh parsley
2 eggs, lightly beaten
4 ½ oz ricotta cheese
9 oz crumbled feta cheese
8 sheets filo pastry
7 tablespoons olive oil
2 cloves garlic, minced
Salt
Pepper

Method of Preparation:

1. Preheat oven to 355F (180 C)
2. In a frying pan, heat 3 tablespoons olive oil and sauté the onions, garlic, spring onions and spinach for about 2 minutes or until spinach is wilted. Add salt and pepper to taste. Set Aside.
3. In a mixing bowl, combine the cheeses, beaten eggs and spinach mixture
4. Oil the baking pan with the remaining olive oil and lay the Filo sheets.

5. Apply oil on the sheets before topping the mixture.
6. Repeat this procedure until four layers are made.
7. Tuck overhanging filo into tin to seal filling.
8. Bake in preheated oven for 30 to 40 minutes until golden brown.

Mushroom, Spinach and Cheese Pie

Seems like pizza but without the mozzarella. And for the crust this recipe uses Filo pastry which gives it a little crisp. You've got mushrooms, onions, spinach and cheeses stuffed inside, giving you an extra appetite.

Yield: Serves 6

Ingredients:
2 large chopped onions
4 cloves garlic, minced
10 oz fresh mushrooms, sliced
10 oz spinach, washed and dried
3 eggs, lightly beaten
1 packet filo pastry
13 oz ricotta cheese
5 ½ oz grated Parmesan cheese
¾ cup soured cream
1.7 oz dried breadcrumbs
Fresh parsley, chopped
4.4 oz butter, melted
2 teaspoons sesame seeds
¼ cup olive oil

Method of Preparation:

1. Preheat oven to 375 F (190 C).
2. Heat oil in a pan then sauté onions and garlic, then add the mushrooms. If it gives out liquid, let it evaporate before adding the Spinach. Let the Spinach wilt for 2 more minutes then set aside.
3. In a separate container, combine cheeses, soured cream, breadcrumbs, parsley and eggs. Add the vegetable mixture draining the excess liquid. Stir until well blended.

4. Oil the baking pan before laying the filo sheets filling.
5. Spread the mixture at the center leaving at least 6-7 inch border. Brush borders with butter.
6. Lay another filo on top of the filling, brushing again with butter. Tuck edges under pie, corners first then the sides.
7. Bake for 40-50 minutes until golden brown. Rest for at least 10 minutes before serving.

Cheesy Mushroom, Pancetta and Spinach Pancakes recipe

When making this recipe, you can use leftover pancakes or you can buy those ready to make pancake boxes at the grocery. The combination of Pancetta and cheeses makes this dish yummy that kids will like. They won't even notice there are greens inside.

Yield: Serves 4

Ingredients:
3 oz cubed pancetta
5 ¼ oz baby chestnut mushrooms, sliced
2 cloves garlic, crushed
18 oz carton fresh four cheese sauce or you can make your cheese sauce
A bunch of baby spinach leaves
Instant pancake mix, 1 box
Parmesan, grated
Fresh parsley

Method of Preparation:

1. Preheat the oven to 390 F (200 C) fan or 355 F (180 C) gas.
2. Prepare your pancakes on a non-stick pan.
3. In a frying pan, heat pancetta until it's brown.
4. Add the garlic, mushrooms and spinach then pour your cheese sauce.
5. Let it simmer for 5 minutes then set aside.
6. Scoop the mixture in each pancake and roll it.
7. Place it in a greased baking pan. Top it with the remaining cheese sauce.
8. Bake for 15 minutes.
9. Garnish with Parmesan and fresh parsley before serving.

Spinach and Goat's Cheese Muffins recipe

These green muffins are packed with vitamins, minerals and proteins from the Spinach and the goat's cheese. The cheese has sour and tangy in flavor but extra delicious in every bite. It's great to have this as sides for soups, breakfast or for snacks.

Yield: Serves 9

Ingredients:
1 oz butter, set aside 5g for greasing
9 oz All Purpose Flour
1 tbsp baking powder
1 tsp bicarbonate of soda
A pinch of cayenne pepper
Parmesan, finely grated
1 egg, lightly beaten
7 oz goat's cheese (rind less)
1 cup milk
Bunch of spinach, washed and stemmed

Method of Preparation:

1. Preheat the oven to 375 F (190C).
2. In a pan, heat butter and half cook the spinach for 1 minute.
3. Chop the Spinach in a food processor and allow cooling. Set aside.
4. Grease the muffin tin with the remaining butter.
5. Sift the flour, bicarbonate of soda and baking powder.
6. Add the cayenne, ground black pepper, parmesan, the egg and the spinach mixture and stir with a wooden spoon. Mix well.
7. Fill in the 9 muffin tins only half full, adding the goat's cheese before filling it up again.

8. Bake for 25-30 minutes until muffins are done.
9. Cool for 5 minutes before serving.

Spinach and Salmon pie

How can anyone think that Omega 3 can now be found in pies? Thanks to this recipe. Now mom's can trick their kids to eat fish without having to force them, and gives them a little extra nutrients from the Spinach too.

Yield: Serves 6

Ingredients:
9 oz All Purpose Flour
4 ½ oz butter, cubed
A pinch of salt
1 tablespoon water
A bunch of fresh spinach
5 oz salmon fillet
salt and pepper to taste
2 cups crème fraiche
1 ½ oz Comte cheese, grated
2 eggs beaten lightly
Olive oil
Salt
Pepper

Method of Preparation:

1. Preheat oven to 390 F (200C).
2. In a mixing bowl, put the flour, butter and water.
3. Using your hands, slowly mix all ingredients together until coarse. Shape into balls and set aside.
4. In a pan, heat olive oil and sauté the spinach.
5. Next, season salmon with salt and pepper. Fry for about 8-10 minutes then crumble.
6. With the beaten eggs, add the crème and mix with a wooden spoon. Add the Comte and salmon to the mixture.

7. Butter the pie dish.
8. Using a rolling pin, flatten the roll and use it to line the pie dish.
9. Pour in the mixture then bake in the oven for 25-30 minutes.

Greek spinach and leek pie

This traditional Greek pie has simple herbs and vegetables such as dill, leeks, parsley, spinach, spring onions, egg whites and mint as ingredients baked to make a one nice pie.

Yield: Serves 9

Ingredients:
1 cup milk
10 oz crumbled feta cheese
4 eggs
14 oz chopped fresh spinach
3 leeks, chopped
a bunch of spring onions, chopped
1 bunch parsley, chopped
1 bunch dill, chopped
1 bunch mint, chopped
1 teaspoon caster sugar
1 cup olive oil
10 oz All purpose flour
3 oz semolina
2 cups water
3 ½ oz grated Parmesan cheese (optional)
4 tablespoons cold butter
salt and ground black pepper

Method of Preparation:

1. Preheat an oven to 355 F (180 C)
2. In a bowl, beat the eggs. Then stir in the spinach, feta cheese, leeks, spring onions, dill, parsley, mint, sugar, milk and ¾ cup of olive oil and mix well.
3. Season with salt and pepper then set aside.

4. In a mixing bowl, combine semolina, APF and salt. Stir in ¼ cup of olive oil and water. Make sure it's lump-free.
5. Pour into battered dish evenly. Spoon the filling and pouring the remaining batter on top.
6. Sprinkle with Parmesan cheese, butter and olive oil before baking.
7. Bake for 50 minutes to 1 hour until browned.

Spinach Beef Spaghetti Pie

This extra meaty pie has a twist - it uses pasta instead of dough as the base for the pie. You can also use cold spaghetti if you have leftover in the refrigerator from yesterday's dinner. Nothing can be wasted, isn't it?

Yield: Serves 9

Ingredients:
6 ounces uncooked angel hair pasta
2 eggs, lightly beaten
1/3 cup parmesan cheese
1 lb ground beef
1/2 cup chopped onion
1/4 cup chopped green pepper
1 (14 ounce) jar meatless sauce
1 teaspoon creole seasoning
3/4 teaspoon garlic powder
1/2 teaspoon basil
1/2 teaspoon oregano
1 (8 ounce) package cream cheese, softened
1 (10 ounce) package frozen spinach, thawed and squeezed dry
1/2 cup shredded mozzarella cheese
2 tablespoons olive oil

Method of Preparation:

1. Boil Angel hair pasta until Al-dente. Run a cold bath to avoid overcooking. Drain well.
2. Add the beaten eggs and Parmesan cheese then transfer to a 9-inch baking pie dish. Make sure the bottom is covered.
3. Scoop the crème cheese on top of the pasta mixture and smoothen it using a spoon.

4. In a sauté pan, heat the olive oil and sauté the onions, bell pepper and beef.
5. Add the oregano, basil and garlic powder.
6. Pour in the sauce and let it simmer for 10 minutes.
7. When the sauce has been reduced, add in the spinach.
8. Pour into the pie dish and top with mozzarella cheese
9. Bake for 20 minutes until golden brown.

Spinach Pie

A very easy Spinach recipe and only takes 30 minutes to prepare and bake. Great for breakfast and snacks.

Yield: serves 4

Ingredients:
10 ounces frozen spinach
1 cup cottage cheese
4 egg whites
1 tbsp Parmesan cheese
½ tsp Garlic powder
2 tsp Salt
1 tsp Pepper
1 tsp Onion powder

Method of Preparation:

1. Preheat oven to 350 degrees F.
2. Combine all ingredients and mix well.
3. Place into a pie dish and bake for 45 minutes until done.

Quick and Easy Spinach Bread

We will use a ready- made pizza crust dough for this recipe, with sautéed spinach filing with garlic, parmesan and Mozzarella cheese stuffing. It's best to serve hot while the cheeses are still bubbly.

Yield: serves 4

Ingredients:
1 tablespoon olive oil
2 cloves garlic, minced
10 oz refrigerated pizza crust dough
10 oz frozen chopped spinach, thawed and drained
1/2 cup grated Parmesan cheese
1/4 tsp Garlic powder
1 cup mozzarella cheese
Salt and pepper

Method of Preparation:

1. Preheat oven to 350 F (175C).
2. In a sauté pan, heat olive oil, then sauté garlic and spinach. Let the liquid evaporate. Set aside.
3. Spread flour on top of a clean surface to avoid sticking, then roll the pizza crust.
4. Then spread spinach mixture evenly on top and add the Mozzarella.
5. Roll to the sides and pinch the seam to seal.
6. Lay on a greased baking pan and bake for about 20-25 minutes.

<u>Mains</u>

Marinated Steak with Spinach and Feta cheese Roulades

The marinade mixture of the meat makes this dish special. Some use it to make a special gravy to pour into the roulades later. Combined with Italian seasoning, it makes this dish more sumptuous and appealing to the taste. Serve hot and enjoy the melted cheese.

Yield: Serves 4

Ingredients:
1 ½ lb beef flank steak or skirt steak, pounded to make rolls and make small slits.
6 tablespoons olive oil
6 tablespoons soy sauce
6 tablespoons red wine
6 tablespoons Worcestershire sauce
2 tablespoons Dijon mustard
2 tablespoons lemon juice
2 clove garlic, minced
1 teaspoon Italian seasoning
1/2 teaspoon ground black pepper
2 cloves garlic, peeled
1/4 teaspoon salt
1 large onion, chopped
6 tablespoons breadcrumbs
1 can frozen chopped spinach, thawed and squeezed dry
2 ½ oz crumbled feta cheese

Method of Preparation:

1. Combine olive oil, soy sauce, Worcestershire sauce, salt, pepper, mustard, lemon juice, Italian seasoning, red wine and garlic in a container or in a reseal able bag and marinade beef overnight. Place in the refrigerator.

2. Preheat oven to 355 F (180 C).
3. In a bowl, combine mixture of spinach, bread crumbs, chopped onions, cheese and garlic, salt and pepper.
4. Spread on the marinated beef and roll to make a roulade. Make sure the roll is secured with skewers and place in a baking dish.
5. Once done, cut roulades ½ inch thick and serve.

Shrimp & Spinach Spring Rolls

A new variety of spring roll filling such as this would boost your appetite even more. This has less fat compared to pork filling and more nutrients. You only need shrimps, carrots, onion, garlic, egg and spring roll wrapper. Great if dipped in Sweet chili sauce.

Yield: Serves 4

Ingredients:
4 oz fresh shrimps, washed, peeled and chopped
1 medium carrot, minced
1 medium onion, chopped
2 cloves garlic, minced finely
Bunch of fresh spinach leaves, washed and cut
6 tablespoons All purpose flour
1 egg beaten (optional)
Breadcrumbs
Cilantro, chopped
½ cup soy sauce
Salt
Ground pepper
4 Spring roll wrappers
1 cup vegetable oil for frying

Method of Preparation:

1. Combine all ingredients in a mixing bowl. For longer lasting spring roll, egg can be optional.
2. Mix everything with a wooden spoon or with your bare hands. Make sure hands are clean.
3. Take 2-3 tablespoon of the filling and put at the near edge of the wrapper to roll. Use water to moisten the edges of the wrapper to hold everything inside. Make sure to wrap it tightly so nothing would spill when deep-frying.

4. In a deep frying pan, heat 1 cup of vegetable oil.
5. Deep fry the rolls until medium brown, over medium heat.
6. Serve with sweet chili sauce.

Spinach Florentine Lasagne

From the word itself, Florentine, this dish is overflowing with Spinach and a whole lot of flavors. Topped with cheeses, it will surely make your mouth water. It's best if served with garlic bread on the side.

Yield: Serves 8

Ingredients:
1 pack lasagne sheets
4 tablespoons butter
1 large red pepper, chopped
3 large onion, chopped
1 can fresh mushrooms, chopped
1 lb small curd cottage cheese
20 oz frozen chopped spinach
Parmesan cheese, grated and divided
1 teaspoon ground black pepper
14 oz passata
2 teaspoons dried marjoram
1 teaspoon caster sugar
1 teaspoon garlic granules
Mozzarella cheese, grated
2 eggs, lightly beaten
Basil, chopped
Parsley, chopped for garnish

Method of Preparation:

1. Preheat oven to 355 F (180 C).
2. Boil the Lasagne sheets until Al-Dente. Set aside.
3. In a saucepan, heat butter and sauté the red pepper, mushrooms and onion until tender.
4. Next, heat passata, sugar, marjoram and garlic granules.

5. In a separate mixing bowl, combine sautéed vegetable mixture, spinach, cottage cheese, eggs, pepper and 4 tablespoons of the Parmesan cheese; mix well.
6. Spread filling in lasagna sheets and place in a baking dish.
7. Top with the remaining cheeses and bake in a preheated oven for 30 mins.
8. Garnish with chopped parsley before serving.

Garlic Sautéed Spinach

This is a 5-minute recipe and very easy to make that you can enjoy doing yourself. Use this recipe as sidings to your favorite main course or if you want to cut down calories, make it as a side for your favorite Fish recipe.

Yield: Serves 4

Ingredients:
A bunch of baby spinach leaves
2 tablespoons olive oil
6 cloves garlic, minced
kosher salt
ground black pepper
1 tablespoon unsalted butter
Lemon

Method of Preparation:

1. Wash spinach and dry using a salad spinner.
2. In a pan, heat olive oil and sauté garlic but do not brown.
3. Add the spinach leaves tossing it in the pan. Add salt and pepper to taste.
4. Immediately place it in a bowl. Squeeze in the lemon before serving.

Poached Eggs Florentine recipe

Originated in Florence, Italy, this dish has an overflowing sauce topped to the eggs and spinach and baked until golden. Not too costly for everyday lunch or dinner which makes it an all-time favorite.

Yield: Serves 4

Ingredients:
1.25 oz plain flour
1 1/3 cup semi-skimmed milk
1.75 oz Gruyère, coarsely grated
2 ½ lb fresh spinach, washed
2.6 oz sunflower margarine
1 tablespoon White wine vinegar
8 fresh eggs
Parsley, chopped

Method of Preparation:

1. To make the sauce, make a roux by heating the butter and adding flour. Stir in for 1 minute to avoid lumps.
2. Pour in the milk in the roux and bring to boil. Set aside.
3. In a separate pan, blanch the spinach and drain. Season with Salt and Pepper.
4. Poach the eggs in a deep saucepan by boiling water and adding 1 tablespoon of vinegar. Stir the eggs carefully for 1 minute in the solution using a slotted spoon. Place the eggs when done in a plate with tissue paper to drain the excess liquid.
5. On a baking dish, place the eggs, top it with the spinach and overflowing sauce and cheese and reheat until cheese are melted. Garnish with parsley.

Spinach Gratin with Hard Boiled Eggs

Treat your family with this creamy recipe topped with hard boiled eggs and gruyere cheese. You can add eggs and cheese as much as you want according to your preference. Add a little more bread crumbs to add more crisp in every bite.

Yield: Serves 6-8

Ingredients:
4 hard boiled eggs, cut
2 cups of milk
A bunch of Spinach, fresh or frozen about 24 ounces, drained
4 tbsp butter
4 tbsp flour
A pinch of freshly grated nutmeg,
Freshly ground black pepper
Gruyere cheese (about 1 ounce)
A handful of bread crumbs
Olive oil

Method of Preparation:

1. Blanche the Spinach for 1 minute and do a cold bath to avoid overcooking. Drain all excess liquid very well. Set aside.
2. To make your béchamel sauce, heat the butter and sprinkle the flour to avoid lumps stirring it constantly. Slowly pour in the milk until it thickens. Bring it to a boil. Add salt, pepper and nutmeg.
3. In a baking pan, pour in the spinach and béchamel mixture, even out the surface.
4. Slice the eggs and top it in the gratin. Top it with the bread crumbs and Gruyere cheese.

5. Drizzle with olive oil before baking for about 25-30 minutes until done.

Easy Spinach Quiche

This easy quiche without a pastry will save you time and effort to prepare. Good for quick breakfast on special days. Sure this recipe is packed with all the energy you need to get you going throughout the day.

Yield: Serves 4

Ingredients:
5 oz Frozen spinach, thawed
2 eggs beaten
9 oz cottage cheese
4 oz grate Cheddar cheese
Spring onions, finely chopped
Olive oil

Method of Preparation:

1. Preheat oven to 320F (160 C)
2. Sauté Spinach in Olive oil for 2 minutes. Drain off excess liquid.
3. Add in eggs, spring onions and cheddar cheese.
4. Pour into quiche dish and back for 30-45 minutes until eggs are done.

Spinach Pasta

A simple but creamy Spinach pasta dish with a treat of bacon bits to make it more appealing.

Yield: Serves 2

Ingredients:
9 oz Pasta of choice
18 oz frozen spinach, pureed
9 oz mild cheese set aside 20g for toppings
2/3 cup heavy cream
A pinch of nutmeg
Olive oil
Bacon bits for garnish
Salt
Pepper

Method of Preparation:

1. In a saucepan, boil your pasta of choice.
2. Drain and drizzle with olive oil to avoid sticking.
3. In a pan, heat olive oil and sauté the spinach.
4. Add in the mild cheese and crème.
5. Season with nutmeg, salt and pepper.
6. Let it simmer for 2 minutes.
7. Using a food processor, puree the mixture.
8. In a plate, put your pasta and ladle the sauce.
9. Top with the remaining cheese and bacon bits.

Seafood and Spinach Risotto

This dish is a well-rounded meal that the whole family can enjoy. It is packed with carbohydrates you need from the rice, Protein, Vitamins and Minerals and a whole lot more from the Spinach. Serve this to your family at least twice a week.

Yield: Serves 4

Ingredients:
3 tablespoons olive oil
1 box (1 lb) Arborio (risotto) rice
4 ¼ cup vegetable stock
14 oz fresh spinach leaves
1 medium leek, chopped
1 fresh red chili, chopped
2 teaspoons finely chopped garlic
14 oz medium prawns, peeled and deveined
7 oz small scallops
1 small red pepper, finely chopped
Fresh ground pepper
Parsley, finely chopped
Salt to taste

Method of Preparation:

1. In a pan, heat the olive oil and pour in the Arborio rice.
2. Stir until every grain is coated with the olive oil.
3. Bit by bit pour in the vegetable stock letting the rice absorb it. Once absorbed, repeat this process until rice is cooked.
4. In a separate pan, sauté garlic, leek, chili, prawns and scallops, spinach and red bell pepper. Season with salt and pepper.
5. Combine the sautéed seafood into the rice and mix well.
6. Garnish with parsley before serving

Healthy Spinach Omelette

This is a very healthy treat to start your day and very easy to make, even kids will enjoy doing this at home. You only need eggs and a handful of spinach. Packed with Calcium and Proteins, this will surely energize your day.

Yield: Serves 2

Ingredients:
4 eggs, lightly beaten
A handful of spinach, washed and torn
Olive oil
½ cup of milk
2 cloves garlic, crushed
1 small Onion, chopped
Grated cheddar cheese

Method of Preparation:

1. In a small pan, heat oil and sauté onions, garlic and spinach for 2 minutes.
2. Immediately pour in your beaten eggs. Let it sit until it's half cooked.
3. Top loads of cheese and let it melt over low heat.
4. Serve with cereals or toast.

Spinach and Artichoke Spaghetti Bake

A vegetarian type of Spaghetti, that is so appealing to the bite but low in calories. Indulge yourself into this Spinach and Artichoke treat without feeling guilty.

Yield: Serves 4

Ingredients:
9 oz spaghetti
2 eggs
9 oz frozen chopped spinach, thawed
8 tablespoons milk
2/3 cup sour cream
Can (12oz) artichoke hearts, drained and chopped
Grated Cheddar cheese
Parmesan cheese, set aside a portion for garnish
1 teaspoon dried onion
salt and pepper to taste
paprika to taste
parsley, finely chopped for garnish

Method of Preparation:

1. Preheat oven to 355 F (180 C).
2. Cook spaghetti noodles in boiling water until al-dente then drain.
3. In a mixing bowl, combine the rest of the ingredients like milk, sour cream, eggs, artichokes, spinach, salt, pepper and paprika.
4. Then add the spaghetti noodles and mix well with the mixture.
5. Transfer contents in a baking dish and top with the grated cheddar cheese and parmesan.
6. Bake for 15-20 minutes.

7. Garnish with parsley and add a little more parmesan on top before serving.

Garlic Chicken Spinach and Orzo

This dish is a complete meal with sautéed chicken, spinach, cheese and pasta. It is loaded with carbohydrates, proteins and calcium. If you want this extra hot, add up a little more chili according to your liking.

Yield: Serves 4

Ingredients:
9 oz uncooked orzo pasta
2 skinless, boneless chicken breast fillets, cut into bite-size pieces
6 tbsps olive oil, 2 tbsps for drizzling
4 cloves garlic
1/4 teaspoon crushed chilies
1 tablespoon fresh parsley, chopped
5.5 oz fresh spinach leaves
Parmesan cheese, grated for toppings
Salt
Pepper

Method of Preparation:

1. Cook Orzo pasta until Al-dente for about 8 minutes.
2. Drain all liquid and drizzle with olive oil to keep it moist.
3. In a sauté pan, heat the remaining olive oil and sauté the garlic, chilies and chicken. Season with salt and pepper.
4. Once chicken is done, add the spinach and continue cooking for about 2-3 minutes until spinach has wilted.
5. Combine orzo with the sautéed vegetable and chicken and sprinkle Parmesan on top.
6. Serve hot.

Chicken Roulade with Cheddar and Spinach

Season the chicken breast when pounding so that flavor would be absorbed before- hand. Add more cheese on top to make it more satisfying. This Roulade is very easy to make and nice to have for dinner with the whole family. NO need for cheese sauce, this recipe is loaded with cheese.

Yield: Serves 4

Ingredients:
10 oz fresh spinach leaves
2/3 cup soured cream
2.5 oz Cheddar cheese, grated
4 cloves garlic, finely chopped
4 boneless chicken breast fillets, skin removed, pounded until thin
Pepper
Salt
8 strips of bacon
2 tablespoons olive oil

Method of Preparation:

1. Preheat the oven to 375 F (190 C)
2. In a sauté pan, heat olive oil and sauté garlic and spinach. Add in soured cream and cheddar cheese.
3. Place chicken breasts in a flat, clean surface and spoon on filings on top of the chicken breasts.
4. Roll the breasts carefully.
5. Wrap in the bacon strips on each roll, securing it with cocktail sticks.
6. Place in a baking dish and bake for 10-15 minutes until done.

Spinach and Ricotta Stuffed Chicken Breasts, with Tomato Sauce

The combination of mozzarella and ricotta cheese makes this dish extra yummy. Baked to perfection, the moist chicken inside is perfect in every bite. Serve with your favorite sides like salad or mashed potato.

Yield: Serves 4

Ingredients:
4 boneless chicken breast fillets, skin removed
14 oz ricotta cheese
9 oz frozen chopped spinach, thawed and drained
2 cloves garlic, finely chopped
2 eggs, lightly beaten
7 oz mozzarella cheese, grated and divided
16 oz pasta sauce
Salt
Pepper
Fresh parsley, for garnish

Method of Preparation:

1. Preheat oven to 355 F (180 C)
2. Season you chicken breasts with salt and pepper. Set aside.
3. In a mixing bowl, combine ricotta cheese, spinach, garlic, eggs, half of the mozzarella cheese.
4. Slit chicken breasts for the stuffing. Fill in each breast.
5. Place in a baking pan. Pour the sauce over and add the remaining mozzarella cheese.
6. Cook for about 20-25 minutes until done.
7. Garnish with fresh parsley before serving

Gnocchi in Gorgonzola Sauce with Spinach and Toasted Walnuts recipe

This delicious and creamy dish would take time to prepare but it's all worth it. If you have left-over mashed potatoes from yesterday's dinner, make it into gnocchi to save money and effort. The walnut gives this dish a crunch and healthy fats while the spinach give its nutritional value and of course delicious flavor.

Yield: Serves 4

Ingredients:
For the potato gnocchi
14 oz potatoes
One egg yolk, lightly whisked
1 cup flour
Pinch of salt

For the rest
7 oz spinach
3.5 oz creamy Gorgonzola cheese
6 tbsp heavy cream
1.5 oz walnut pieces
1 oz grated Parmesan

Method of Preparation:

1. Boil and mash the potatoes.
2. Add eggs, flour and a pinch of salt to the mashed potatoes and kneed into a dough.
3. Roll the potato dough into ¾ inch then cutting it into ½ inch pieces, slightly pinch the center of each piece.
4. Boil the potato gnocchi for 4-5 minutes or wait until it floats.

5. Gather with a slotted spoon and place in a plate. Set aside.
6. In a baking dish, grill the walnuts until slightly toasted for 5 minutes.
7. In a pan, combine the gorgonzola cheese, heavy cream and parmesan and bring it to a boil.
8. Add the spinach into the sauce and stir, then the gnocchi.
9. In a baking dish, pour contents and bake for 10-15 minutes until golden.
10. Before serving, top with the toasted walnuts.

Soba Noodle Soup with Spinach and Smoked Trout

This recipe is a balanced meal and is packed with Carbohydrates, Proteins, Vitamins and Minerals. It's best for cold weathers, especially when you feel you want Asian food but can't go out. You've got Soba noodles, Trout, Spinach and scallions all in one dish. Grab a pair of chopsticks and enjoy.

Yield: Serves 3

Ingredients:
5 cups vegetable or chicken stock
4 ounces Japanese soba noodles
1/2 pound smoked trout fillets, skinned and cut into portions
Soy sauce to taste
1 tablespoon sesame oil
4 ounces baby spinach
1 bunch of scallions, sliced
White pepper

Method of Preparation:

1. In a saucepan, heat water and add the soba noodles. Bring to a boil until soba noodles are cooked, adding more water if it gets dried up.
2. Heat the vegetable stock and season with soy sauce and white pepper. Add the trout.
3. Distribute the noodles evenly to 3 bowls, adding the spinach and scallions. Ladle in the stock with the trout. Add in sesame oil.

Spinach, Sausage and Cheese Bake

A special dish that's like pizza but without a crust, overloaded with Spinach and topped with 3 kinds of Cheeses, you surely wouldn't want to miss a dinner that has this dish on the table. By the way, who's got hot sauce?

Yield: Serves 6-8

Ingredients:
1 pound Italian sausage, Chopped
20 ounces frozen chopped spinach, thawed and drained
8 ounce can tomato sauce
2 cups cottage cheese
1 cup grated Parmesan cheese
1 cup shredded mozzarella cheese
1 egg, beaten
Salt
Pepper
Parsley, finely chopped
1 tablespoon butter

Method of Preparation:

1. Preheat oven to 355 F (180 C).
2. In a frying pan, heat butter and fry the Italian sausage. Discard any excess fat. Set aside.
3. Combine the cheeses, setting aside a little mozzarella for toppings, egg, spinach and tomato sauce.
4. In a baking dish, pour the contents and top with the Italian sausage and extra cheese.
5. Bake for 20-25 minutes until bubbly. Sprinkle with fresh parsley before serving.

Creamy Spinach Casserole

An all-time favorite, this recipe is somewhat similar to what we order in restaurants. The dish gets its flavor from the cream of mushroom soup. Allow to reduce to avoid a watery casserole. Serve hot.

Yield: Serves 8-10

Ingredients:
1 can condensed cream of mushroom soup
20 ounces frozen chopped spinach, thawed and drained
7 oz chicken breast chopped into pieces
1 red onion, diced finely
4 tablespoons butter
½ teaspoon garlic salt
½ cup Parmesan cheese
salt and pepper to taste
extra mushrooms (optional)

Method of Preparation:

1. In a saucepan, add the butter and sauté the onion.
2. Add chicken pieces when the onion becomes transparent.
3. When the chicken is done add everything else and simmer until it becomes the desired thickness.
4. When it thickens then remove from heat and serve.

Pizza with Garlic, Spinach & Mozzarella

A vegetarian pizza that uses pita bread instead of crust for an extra crisp. You can add more of your favorite vegetables like broccoli, mushrooms, bell peppers or Pineapple and will only take 10 minutes o cook. Everybody just loves pizza!

Yield: Serves 8-10

Ingredients:
2/3 cup tomato sauce
2 whole wheat pitas
3 cloves garlic, finely minced
1 cup spinach
2 oz fresh mozzarella (sliced into round shapes)
5 fresh basil leaves
2 tbsps of oregano
1/2 tsp red pepper flakes (optional)

Method of preparation:

1. Preheat oven to 400 F
2. In a bowl, combine the tomato sauce, garlic, oregano and pepper flakes
3. Lay pita in a baking sheet and spread the sauce using a spoon.
4. Top with the rest of the ingredients and the cheese, then bake for 10-15 minutes.

Salads

Spinach and Mango salad

Your typical Spinach salad with a taste of fruit from the orient will surely awaken your taste buds. Surely you'll want more of the sweet-acidic taste of the fruit, not to mention cutting down on calories. You only need Spinach, Mangoes, almonds and your vinaigrette.

Yield: Serves 6

Ingredients:
1 bunch of fresh spinach, washed, torn and spin-dried
4 mangos - peeled and diced
7 oz flaked almonds
8 tablespoons red wine vinegar
4 tablespoons balsamic vinegar
4 tablespoons olive oil
2 dessertspoon mustard powder
Handful of chopped fresh tarragon
Salt
Freshly ground black pepper
4 Mangos - peeled and diced

Method of Preparation:

1. Preheat oven to 300 F
2. Toast flaked almonds until fragrant for 15 - 20 minutes.
3. Place the spinach and mangoes in a salad bowl
4. In a small bowl, combine balsamic vinegar. Olive oil, red wine vinegar, mustard powder. Mix well then pour into the salad greens.
5. Garnish with the toasted almonds and serve.

Asian Spinach Salad with Chicken, Mushrooms, Peppers, and Almond

The ginger puree makes this salad more "Asian" aside from Sesame oil which is often used in Ramen. It would take an hour including preparation to do this salad, but it's all worth the effort.

Yield: Serves 3-4

Ingredients:
2 boneless chicken breasts, skin removed, cut into strips
A bunch of spinach, washed and spin-dried
1 cup sliced pepper strips (choose any color you want or a combination)
1/4 cup almonds
6 oz. mushrooms, sliced
3 pcs green onions, sliced
A bunch of spinach, washed and spin-dried

Dressing Ingredients:
3 tablespoons rice vinegar
2 tablespoons soy sauce
3 tablespoons olive oil
1/4 tsp. ginger puree
2 tsp sugar
1/2 tsp. sesame oil
¼ - 1/2 tsp. Sriracha Sauce (or more if you want it spicy)
salt
pepper

Method of Preparation:

1. Season chicken breasts with salt and pepper, then grill or fry in a pan.
2. Toast almonds for about 5 minutes until medium brown.

3. Sauté mushrooms and bell pepper strips in olive oil. Do not overcook.
4. In a mixing bowl, combine rice vinegar, olive oil, soy sauce, ginger puree, sugar, Sriracha sauce and sesame oil.
5. Toss together the spinach and sautéed vegetables, pouring the salad dressing.

Warm Beet and Spinach salad

A colorful salad with touches of green, red and black that is often served with the beet still warm. A nice combination of the beet, spinach, olives, tomatoes, onions in olive oil and balsamic vinegar. A favorite starter for special dinners.

Yield: Serves 4

Ingredients:
8 cups baby spinach, washed and spin-dried
2 cups steamed beet, ½ inch thick
2 tablespoon extra-virgin olive oil
1 cup thinly sliced red onion
2 tomatoes, chopped
2 tablespoons sliced olives
2 tablespoons chopped fresh parsley
2 clove garlic, minced
2 tablespoons balsamic vinegar
Salt

Method of Preparation:

1. In a skillet, heat olive oil and sauté onions until translucent.
2. Add the tomatoes, olives, garlic and parsley.
3. Then later add the beet.
4. When it's done wait for 2 minutes to cool a bit.
5. In a salad bowl, place the spinach and top with the sautéed vegetable, vinegar and salt.
6. Toss and serve hot.

Spinach and Citrus Salad

A citrusy salad packed with Proteins, vitamin C and E and a lot more. You can substitute grapefruit with oranges in case of unavailability or for a lighter flavor.

Yield: Serves 4

Ingredients:
8 cups fresh spinach leaves, washed, spin-dried and torn
1 small red onion, thinly sliced
2 small grapefruit, skin removed and cut into 8 pieces
1 tablespoon white-wine vinegar
1 tablespoon extra-virgin olive oil
1/2 tablespoon coarse-grain mustard
1/2 teaspoon honey
1 clove garlic, minced chopped
1/4 teaspoon salt
Freshly ground pepper to taste
1 teaspoon poppy seeds

Method of Preparation:

1. In a small bowl, juice 1 slice of grapefruit and add vinegar, oil, mustard, honey, garlic, salt and pepper.
2. In a salad bowl put the spinach leaves, onions and the grapefruit and add the dressing of the small bowl over it. Toss and serve.

Spinach, Avocado & Mango Salad

Now Avocados are a good source of healthy cholesterol and also very high in Potassium. With added flavor and a unique taste, this light starter would boost your appetite for the main entrée.

Yield: Serves 4

Ingredients:
10 cups baby spinach leaves
1 bunch or 10 small red radishes sliced
1 small ripe mango, sliced
1 medium avocado, sliced
1/4 orange juice
1 1/2 tablespoon red-wine vinegar
2 tablespoons canola oil
1 teaspoon Dijon mustard
1/4 teaspoon salt
Freshly ground pepper

Method of Preparation:

1. Combine orange juice, red wine vinegar, canola oil, Dijon mustard, salt and pepper in a salad bowl.
2. Toss in the spinach leaves, radishes, mango and avocado then serve.

Smoothies

Simple Banana Spinach Smoothie

A smoothie recipe that is so easy to make for kids and adults to enjoy. You only need bananas, orange juice and spinach. Grab a food processor and you're done in 5 minutes.

Yield: Serves 2

Ingredients
3 cups orange juice
3 bananas
2 handful Spinach, washed

Method of Preparation:

1. In a blender put in all the ingredients.
2. Blend until smooth.

Mango, Banana and Spinach Smoothie

These tropical fruits, when blended together, create a wonderful smoothie.

Yield: Serves 2

Ingredients
2 cups cold water
3 handful baby spinach leaves
1 ½ cups frozen mango (frozen)
1 banana (frozen)

Method of Preparation:

1. In a blender put in all the ingredients.
2. Blend until smooth.

Peanut Butter Banana Spinach Smoothie

The peanut butter gives this smoothie a nutty taste that is so addicting, and you'll keep asking for more.

Yield: Serves 3

Ingredients:
2 cups milk
2 cups baby spinach
2 bananas
2 tbsp creamy peanut butter

Method of Preparation:

1. In a blender put in all the ingredients.
2. Blend until smooth.

Pineapple Mango Spinach Smoothie

With all these delicious fruits you'll get plenty of fiber and together with the spinach makes it a really unique tasting delicious smoothie.

Yield: Serves 2
Ingredients:
3/4 cup pineapple juice
1 cup cold water
1/2 cup mango
1 cup green grapes (frozen)
1 banana (frozen)
2 handfuls baby spinach (organic)

Method of Preparation:

1. In a blender put in all the ingredients.
2. Blend until smooth.

Orange Blueberry Banana Spinach Smoothie

A new flavor to enjoy, with citrus, spinach and berries which has a lot of antioxidants that prevent Cancer. Then Bananas has loads of Potassium. What a great combo!

Yield: Serves 2
Ingredients:
2 cup orange juice
2 handful baby spinach
2 bananas
1 cup blueberries

Method of Preparation:

1. In a blender put in all the ingredients.
2. Blend until smooth.

Other

Basil and Spinach Summer Pesto

These abundant herbs are blended to perfection and can be used as sauce for your pasta, or can be used as spread to your bread. Store it properly and you can use this for a week or two.

Yield: Serves 8

Ingredients:
2 garlic cloves, minced
1 oz fresh basil leaves
1.75 oz fresh flat-leaf parsley leaves
1 oz fresh spinach leaves
1.5 oz chopped fresh oregano
2 oz toasted pine nuts
1.5 oz grated Parmesan cheese
1 pinch salt and freshly ground black pepper to taste
¾ cup olive oil

Method of Preparation:

1. Blend all ingredients, filling the food processor halfway only to avoid spillage.
2. Store in an air-tight container and refrigerate.

Made in the USA
Monee, IL
18 October 2024

68285564R00050